50 TIPS TO IMPROVE YOUR SPORTS PERFORMANCE

SEE IT. SAY IT. DO IT!®

DR. LYNN F. HELLERSTEIN

WHAT PEOPLE ARE SAYING ABOUT SEE IT. SAY IT. DO IT!®

"One of the most important ways to separate yourself from others is your ability to utilize visualization techniques. Many of the best athletes in the world, in all sports, have already seen themselves executing the fundamentals of their sport long before they even get on the court or the field. They understand the importance of their visualization process. Dr. Hellerstein has found a way to explain these and many other keys in a simple, easy-to-read format. Well worth the time invested to read *50 Tips to Improve Your Sports Performance!*"

Kevin Eastman
Assistant Coach, Boston Celtics

"Having worked with amateur and professional athletes alike, *See It. Say It. Do It!* is a must-read for all individuals involved in meaningful movement. The information, techniques and activities benefit our children on every level of life's learning journey."

Sue Lowe, O.D., FAAO, FCOVD
Past Chair of the American Optometric Association Sports Vision Section

"*See It. Say It. Do It!* has been instrumental in developing my skills in yoga and gymnastics, as well as in my professional practice. Each step of the process is essential to achieving lifestyle changes. My clients experience long-lasting behavior changes when we follow the process. Thank you Dr. Hellerstein for providing the tools and framework to change lives. We celebrate the *Ta-Dahs!*"

Rebecca Simon
Registered Dietician and Wellness Coach

"Ground breaking! *50 Tips to Improve Your Sports* is a must-read for any person looking to enhance their sports performance. Visualize getting this book today... now take action and get it!"

James Malinchak
Featured on ABC's Hit TV Show, "Secret Millionaire,"
Co-Author, Chicken Soup for the College Soul

"*Visualize!* Dr. Hellerstein's book, *See It. Say It. Do It!*, was my mantra as I took on the challenge of Nepal's Everest Base Camp at 17,500 feet. Chapter six of *See It. Say It. Do It!* described how Dr. Hellerstein prepared for the challenge of her first marathon. This greatly helped me prepare for my trek."

Terry Zelenak RN, BSN, CHPN
Hospice and Palliative Care

 www.HiClearPublishing.com
Greenwood Village, Colorado

© 2013, 2014 by Lynn Hellerstein. All rights reserved. No part of this book may be reproduced in any written, electronic, recording, or photocopying form without written permission of the publisher. The exception would be in the case of brief quotations embodied in critical articles or reviews and pages where permission is specifically granted by the publisher. Although every precaution has been taken to verify the accuracy of the information contained herein, the author and publisher assume no responsibility for any errors or omissions. No liability is assumed for damages that may result from the use of information contained within.

SEE IT. SAY IT. DO IT!® is a registered trademark of
Hellerstein Resources for Creative Learning, LLC.

Books may be purchased for sales promotion and for volume pricing
by contacting the publisher:

HiClear Publishing, LLC,
7400 E. Orchard Road, Suite 175-S
Greenwood Village, CO 80111
303-850-9499 • 303-850-7032 Fax • Info@HiClearPublishing.com

Design by Annie Harmon, *Harmony Design, LLC*
Illustrations by Shannon Parish, *IllustratingYou, LLC*

LCCN: 2012918702
ISBN: 978-0-9841779-4-3

1. Sports.   2. Sports Vision.   3. Athletes.   4. Vision training.

Second Printing
Printed in the United States

LINE-UP

TABLE OF CONTENTS

	Introduction	1
Part One	Eye-Mind-Body Coordination	5
Part Two	Achieve the Mental Edge Through the SEE IT. SAY IT. DO IT!® Process	27
Part Three	Eye/Vision Safety	59
	About the Author	69

YES NO

- ☐ ☐ Are you inconsistent in your performance during a game or sporting event?

- ☐ ☐ Do you lose concentration during sports performance?

- ☐ ☐ Is it hard to keep your eyes accurately tracking?

- ☐ ☐ Have you noticed difficulty with depth perception?

- ☐ ☐ Do you use visualization or imagery strategies?

- ☐ ☐ Do you miss your shots or swings?

If you answered YES to any of these questions, then read on...

WARM-UP
INTRO

Athletes of all ages and levels of competition spend a lot of money on sports equipment, training and clothing. You hit the weight room, work on speed and agility, train for hours. But if you picked up this book, you may still not be where you want to be. Something is missing. Mediocre and poor sports performances are not always caused by bad equipment, weakness or reduced speed. Did you ever think that your vision may be holding you back from your peak performance? And if it is, what might you do to improve your vision skills?

Each sport requires specific strength, muscles, speed and movement skills. The same is true about your vision skills. In so many sports, like tennis, baseball, and hockey, split-second decisions make the difference. Exceptional visual skills are one of the keys that separate high performing athletes from average ones. Multiple studies have shown that professional athletes have better visual skills than non-athletes.

Sports vision training provided by optometrists is the new frontier for developing peak athletic skills. You can improve your visual skills to be more efficient and accurate.

50 Tips to Improve Your Sports Performance is dedicated to you: the athlete who wants to perform at your peak potential. Whether you are a weekend warrior or an elite athlete, superior visual skills can take you from "good" to "great," allowing you to increase your potential and maximize your sports performance.

Sports provide life lessons.

Sports and other types of performances are training grounds for life. Beyond the skill of the activity, the lessons you learn are endless: teamwork, leadership, commitment, physical strength, motivation, preparation, mental toughness and confidence. You may not always experience a Ta-Dah! But with continued practice, learning and support, you will develop into a more powerful person. It is about picking yourself up when you fall down. That's a Ta-Dah!

"A champion is a person who fulfills his or her potential and lives a life of satisfaction and service."

Bee Epstein-Shepherd, Ph.D., D.C.H.
Author of Building Champions: A Guide for Parents of Jr. Golfers

PART 1
••• EYE-MIND-BODY •••
COORDINATION

Are you truly able to see, track, focus and concentrate to excel at your sport?

Do you sometimes feel disconnected from what you see and how your body moves?

Vision refers to seeing, processing and responding to visual information. It is impossible to consistently hit a baseball with your eyes closed. If you are a golfer, you can't putt accurately if you have double vision. Enhancing your vision through training parallels what athletes do to develop their strength and movement skills.

Your eyes are truly essential in informing the brain about movement and in using the mind for learning. And it's no surprise kids and adults struggle when they have unresolved vision issues.

TIP #1 Vision is our dominant sense.

Vision engages much of the brain. So training your vision is training your brain, not your eyeballs. Athletes at the top of their game have improved their vision by training.

> "Vision trumps all other senses."
> ***Dr. John Medina***
> *Developmental Biologist, Author of Brain Rules*

TIP #2 Eyesight—20/20 isn't always perfect.

20/20 just means that you can see a small letter about 1-inch tall at 20 feet. You could see double and still have 20/20 vision.

> "20/20 is average vision; athletes should strive for 'optimal' vision, which can be more than twice as good as 20/20."
> ***Dr. Lynn F. Hellerstein***
> *Developmental Optometrist, Sports Vision Authority*

TIP #3 **Great sports performance requires at least 15 vision-related skills to improve visual awareness, reaction time, anticipation and timing.**

- ✓ Visual acuity (clearness of sight)
- ✓ Eye coordination at distance
- ✓ Eye coordination at near
- ✓ Depth perception
- ✓ Eye tracking
- ✓ Sustained focus at far
- ✓ Sustained focus at near
- ✓ Fixation accuracy
- ✓ Peripheral vision
- ✓ Color perception
- ✓ Gross visual-motor coordination
- ✓ Fine visual-motor coordination
- ✓ Visual perception
- ✓ Visual localization
- ✓ Speed of visual recognition

TIP #4 Visual skills can be improved through sports vision training.

Sports vision training improves eye-mind-body-coordination so you can see quicker, respond faster. Training techniques may be very simple activities or involve more complex equipment like those below.

Some athletes might have significant visual problems and should first see an optometrist to resolve some of the more complex difficulties. Glasses, contact lenses or sport vision training may be very beneficial.

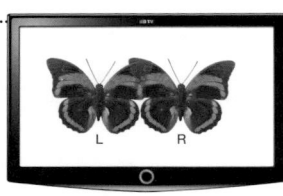

Computer Orthoptics
Liquid Crystal
Automated Vision
Therapy System

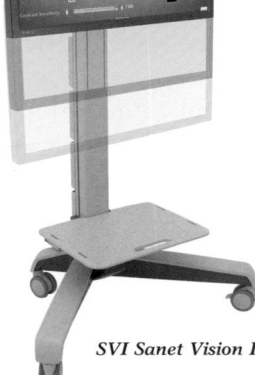

SVI Sanet Vision Integrator

Developed by Robert B. Sanet, OD, FCOVD
and Rodney K. Bortel. htsvision.com

TIP #5 — EYE TRACKING

Eye calisthenics

1. Breathe in and look straight ahead.

2. Breathe out and look as far up as possible, and hold that position for several seconds.

3. Breathe in and look straight ahead.

4. Breathe out and now look as far to the right as possible, and hold that position for several seconds.

5. Breathe in and look straight ahead.

6. Breathe out and look to your far left, again holding for several seconds.

7. Repeat this series of exercises, looking in all directions. Continue to breathe in while looking straight ahead, and then breathe out while holding your gaze in each direction. "Stretch" as far as possible. You may feel discomfort at first, which often improves with time and practice. Do these calisthenics at least twice a day for several minutes each time.

 EYE TRACKING

Figure eights

Keep your head still: these are eye movements, not head movements. Clasp your hands together (see figure) and hold your thumb (or an object) directly in front of your nose, about fourteen to sixteen inches from your face. While keeping your eyes focused on your thumbs, slowly move your thumbs in these patterns: start with left/right movements, then up/down movements and then diagonal movements. Now move your thumbs in a circle, and then in a figure-eight. If this movement hurts or creates discomfort or nausea, consult your optometrist.

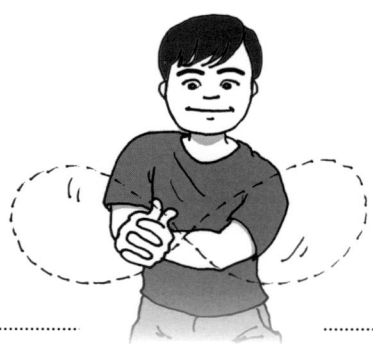

TIP #7 — EYE TRACKING

Eyes on the ball

Do you have trouble catching the ball (or coach athletes who do)? Use a softball for older athletes or a beanbag for younger ones. Apply numbers to the ball/bag by writing or using stickers. Tell the athlete, "Carefully watch the ball and tell me what letter you see." After the athlete has visually fixated on the ball/bag, slowly throw it, encouraging the athlete to look for the specific target on the ball. End result? "Good eye," shouts the coach!

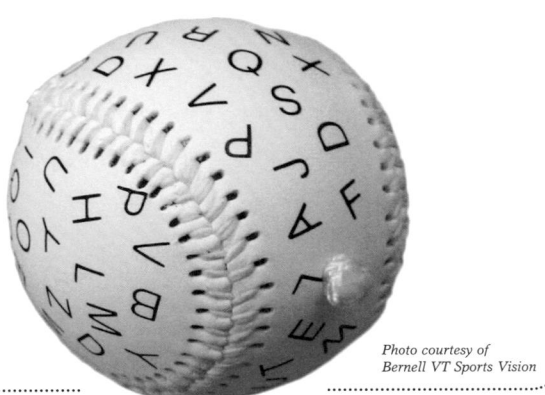

Photo courtesy of Bernell VT Sports Vision

TIP #8 — FOCUS & EYE COORDINATION

The keys to accurate visual information.

For your eyes to work well together as a team, your focus and eye coordination skills must be excellent. You need to be able to quickly and accurately fixate on a target object, then switch between near and far objects.

For example, a baseball pitcher must be able to focus on the glove of the catcher, then shift focus to the base runner. A soccer player may misjudge when to kick the ball, or a basketball player may shoot too early or too late, because of poor focus and eye coordination. If there is a mismatch or inconsistency in these skills, then you receive inaccurate information as to where and when you need to move.

"When shooting, you cannot hit the target if you do not see it correctly. Vision therapy helped me really SEE IT and as a result, I was able to take my game to the next level."

Phil Kiner
Twenty-eight-time Amateur Trapshooting Association All-American and World Record Holder with two 400x400 All-Around Scores

FOCUS & EYE COORDINATION

String & beads

In this exercise, you'll train your eyes using a string and beads held up to your face. Put two beads on a six-foot string. Tie one end to a doorknob or have someone hold it. String the beads so one will be about four inches away from your face when you hold the string up to your nose, and the other bead will be about twenty inches away.

Now hold your end of the string at the bridge of your nose. Look at the near bead. Keep that bead single. You should see two strings, as though one was coming from each eye. If your fixation on the bead is accurate, the strings should appear to cross directly through the center of the bead, forming an "X" pattern with the center of the "X" in focus.

Now look at the distant bead. You should again see an "X" made by the strings, with the center of the "X" crossing through the distant bead. You should also see two near beads.

Jump your focus back and forth between the distant bead and near bead. Always be aware of the strings, the clarity of the beads and strings, and the visual and physical stress this activity may cause. If you don't see an "X," the strings intermittently disappear, or the bead appears doubled, then you may have an eye coordination problem. You should then schedule a vision exam with a sports vision optometrist.

Add more challenge:
Put the string in different locations specific to your sport and still try to see the "X." For example, a golfer may want to place the end of the string towards the ground where the golf ball sits. A basketball or volleyball player may want to tie the end of the string to the basketball hoop on top of the net. Jump and move as you use the string to make sure both eyes are staying focused and coordinated.

ACTIVITY — **TIP #10**

FIXATION ACCURACY

Quick looks

Practice how to quickly look, focus and stay focused... now switch targets!

Hold two pens of different colors about 10 inches apart, about 14-16 inches from your face. Call out the color of one of the pens. Look at the one you called and continue looking until you call out the second color. Then look at the second pen. Repeat the exercise but periodically change the location of one of the pens. Practice this for your entire visual field. Keep your fixation on the pen without being distracted. Notice if you anticipate your next target or take several jumps to locate the pen you want to focus on.

TIP #11
PERIPHERAL VISION
Do you have eyes in the back of your head?

When a basketball player sees a teammate out of the corner of his eye, the player is using his peripheral vision. You can increase your ability to see action to the side without turning your head.

"Ninety-seven percent of vision is peripheral. In many sports situations, especially team sports, processing of information from peripheral vision is an essential element of successful performance. Peripheral vision is critical to generate accurate eye movements, maintain optimal balance and guide the best motor responses."

Graham Erickson, O.D., FAAO, FCOVD
*Professor at Pacific University College of Optometry,
Author of Sports Vision: Vision Care for the
Enhancement of Sports Performance*

ACTIVITY **TIP #12**

PERIPHERAL VISION
Soft focus

Hold the star (on page 19) at reading distance. Look "hard" at the dot in the center, and notice how the dot reduces in size and your awareness of your periphery decreases. Now look "soft" at the dot and notice how your periphery opens up. While looking at the dot, with your finger touch each number in order. Be sure to continue looking at the dot while you touch each number in your periphery.

"At the age of 62, I found it impossible tracking a baseball. After two months of sports vision therapy, I attended a Professional Baseball Fantasy Camp. As the second oldest person attending, I batted .333 and had no fielding errors. I had the time of my life!"

Rick Pfaffmann
Amateur Baseball Player

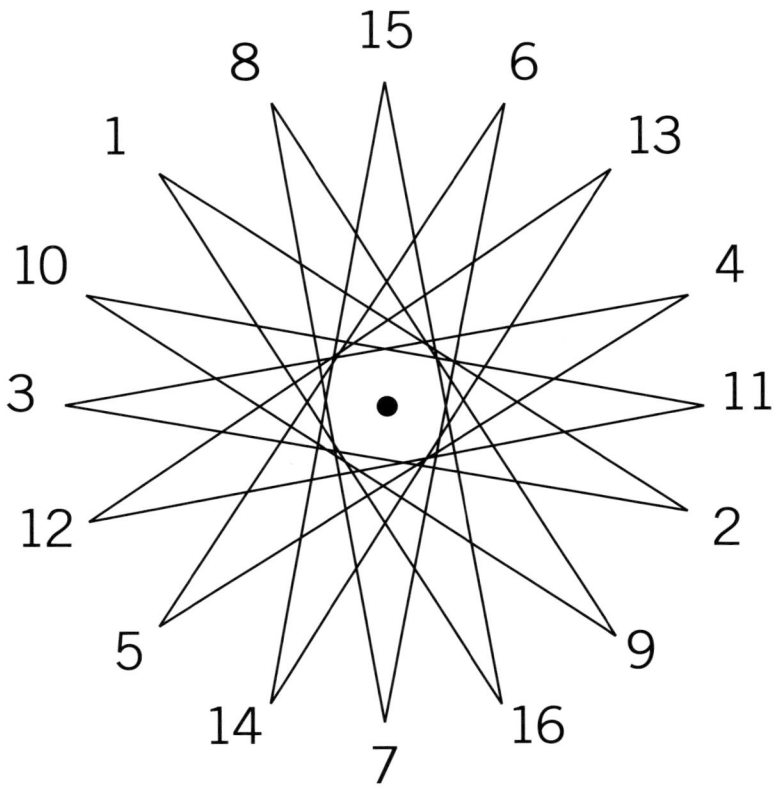

TIP #13

DEPTH PERCEPTION
3D Vision

Depth perception allows you to accurately judge distances and quickly react. Good depth perception is dependent on good eyesight, focusing and eye coordination skills. For example, in tennis, the better your depth perception, the quicker you can accurately know where to move and when to swing at the ball.

> "Roller Derby is obviously a very physical game. It is a very fast-paced sport, and requires confidence and split-second visual decision making."
>
> ***Margot Atwell***
> *Em Dash of Gotham Girls Roller Derby, Vice-Captain of Manhattan Mayhem and member of the All-Stars Team*

TIP #14 EYE-MIND-BODY COORDINATION
Your eyes lead your body.

Vision is the signal that starts the muscles of the body to respond. All sports involving a ball or quick body movements require excellent eye-mind-body coordination. When you drop a ball or miss a swing, what could be happening? It's not necessarily "bad hands" but inaccurate visual input to your body.

> "The great baseball hitters, including Ted Williams, attributed much of their hitting success to picking up the pitcher's release point, seeing the rotation of the ball, and waiting to swing until the very last moment."
>
> ***Bruce Hellerstein***
> *Curator of The National Ballpark Museum, recognized by Smithsonian Institute as One of the Finest Baseball Collections in the World. www.BallparkMuseum.com*

TIP #15

EYE-MIND-BODY COORDINATION
Arrow jump

Draw a series of arrows (see page 23). Standing, move your arms in the direction of the first arrow and call out that direction. Then move your fixation to the next arrow on the right. Again, move your hands in the direction of the arrow and call out that direction. Continue through the entire sheet.

To add difficulty, repeat the activity above, but also jump in the direction of the arrow instead of moving your arms. For arrows pointing up, jump forward. For arrows pointing down, jump backwards.

Add more challenge:
- Use a metronome (a musical tool that helps keep the beat and rhythm) and move your arms or jump to the beat. You can get a metronome at a music store or look online for free downloads of metronomes.

- Change the direction you read the arrows. Instead of left to right, read top to bottom.
- Act in the opposite direction of the arrow. For example, say/move/jump right for a left arrow while saying "left."
- Do the activity on a mini-trampoline.

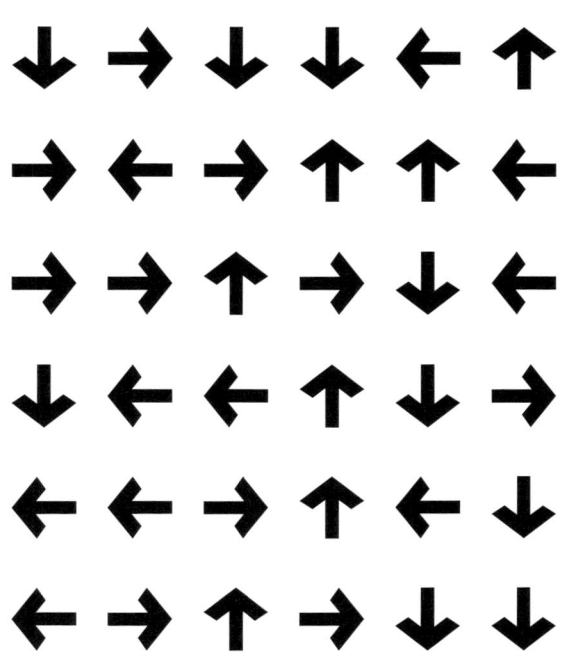

TIP #16 EYE-MIND-BODY COORDINATION

Cross marches

Start marching in place. When your left knee is raised, use your right hand to touch your left knee. When your right knee is raised, use your left hand to touch your right knee. Now continue marching and talk to people around you, always making sure you are using the crossed marching pattern.

TIP #17
EYE-MIND-BODY COORDINATION
NIKE Vapor Strobes

NIKE has created a special training tool for athletes dubbed "Vapor Strobes." These glasses flash microscopic electric charges, blocking vision in 100-millisecond patterns. As you run drills, the lenses flicker between clear and opaque; these distractions force you to anticipate what is coming and focus on your task. This training helps you see things more quickly and accurately...like a running back finding an open hole, a quarterback spotting a free receiver, or a wide receiver watching the ball come into his hands. Find out more about NIKE Vapor Strobes from your sports vision optometrist.

"By giving them less information, we force athletes to utilize what we give them more efficiently. It's essentially stress training on the sensory system."

Dr. Alan Reichow
Professor Emeritus - Pacific University, College of Optometry
Nike Global Research Director: Vision Sciences

PART 2

ACHIEVE THE MENTAL EDGE THROUGH THE
SEE IT. SAY IT. DO IT!®
PROCESS

Do you frequently visualize, or "mentally rehearse," your sports skills?

Most athletes are turning to visualization training to take their game to the next level. How about you?

Pro-golfer Phil Mickelson, Olympic Champion Swimmer Amy Van Dyken, Ice Hockey Champion Wayne Gretsky, World Boxing Champion Muhammad Ali, National Basketball Most Valuable Player Michael Jordan, Olympic Champion Snowboarder Shaun White and many other Olympic and professional athletes all acknowledge that using visualization techniques has allowed them to achieve peak performance.

TIP #18 Visualization impacts your life!

As an athlete, if you want to maximize your physical strengths and skills, you must train your thoughts and ability to visualize. Visualization, often referred to as mental rehearsal or guided imagery, can maximize the efficiency and effectiveness of your training. It's one way to gain that "slim edge."

Visualization is used by many of the greatest athletes in all sports. There is an old saying, "I need to see it to believe it." It goes both ways: "I need to believe it to see it!"

Visualization is about seeing outside and within.

Athletes have their own personal ways to prepare for their sports. Some just show up without any practice, warm-up or preparation. Many great athletes have a routine. What's your routine? Create one that gets you prepared physically, mentally and visually.

TIP #19 SEE IT. SAY IT. DO IT!®

See It *Visualize*
+ **Say It** *Declare*
+ **Do It** *Take Action*
___
Ta-Dah! *Transform*

The SEE IT. SAY IT. DO IT!® process has three parts that make a great pre-sports routine. The order of the components is not critical. However, experience shows that all three parts will produce the greatest result or **Ta-Dah!**

You'll learn all you need to get started in this chapter. For more details, refer to *See It. Say It. Do It!® The Parent's & Teacher's Action Guide to Creating Successful Students & Confident Kids.*
(HiClear Publishing LLC, 2012)

SEE IT. SAY IT. DO IT!

TIP #20 VISUALIZE

See It!

Visualization is the ability to form, imagine, sense, become aware of, move, manipulate and expand the pictures in your "mind's eye," thereby developing new perspectives and creativity.

Key strategies to enhance your visualization:

- ✓ Relax
- ✓ Breathe
- ✓ Build awareness

"Being a marathon runner, mental focus and visualization is necessary and is as big a part of my training and actual marathon as the physical. My mantra is, *My mind controls my body, my body does not control my mind.*"

Jim Lynch
Author of One Foot in Front of the Other

TIP #21 VISUALIZE
The skills & benefits of visualization are valuable in many areas of your life.

- ✓ Mentally practice specific skills
- ✓ Improve confidence
- ✓ Increase problem solving
- ✓ Reduce stress and anxiety
- ✓ Prepare for performance
- ✓ Maintain mental readiness even during injury recovery

"Every day before, I would see an outline of what I knew the future would hold for me. I would feel the environment and visualize the surroundings that would encompass my every action when my moment to shine came. In almost every race that I have implemented this, I have come out victorious."

Sven Lundell
Wyoming State High School Swimming Champion

TIP #22 VISUALIZE
Relax, breathe and build awareness.

It sounds simple, but how often do you notice your shoulders feel tight and scrunched, or your breathing seems fast and shallow? The more you consciously practice to relax, breathe and build awareness, the more automatic these skills become—even in a last-minute, pressured situation.

Stress and anxiety can adversely affect performance across all levels of athletic ability and types of sports. Relaxing is one of the key skills you need to overcome the stress and anxiety you may experience when trying to improve your sports performance. Sounds easy to do, until the competition starts!

ACTIVITY TIP #23 — VISUALIZE

Relax

Find a quiet, comfortable place to lie down or sit. Rest comfortably, and gently allow your eyes to close. Start this exercise by squeezing and releasing specific muscles. First, clench your fists, continue tightening, and then unclench them. Next, tighten your legs; now let them go. Scrunch up your face tight, tighter, tighter! Now relax your face. Go through each body part, tightening, then relaxing. Now make all parts of your body as tight as you can and count to five. Relax your whole body by letting your muscles go soft. How do your muscles feel when they are all tight? What does it feel like when they relax? Continue playing this game, refining which muscles to tighten and then relax.

TIP #24 — VISUALIZE
When all else fails, just breathe.

Breathing deeply creates calmness, which is part of the relaxation process that aids visualization. Just one deep breath can help reduce anxiety, panic attacks, irritability, muscle tension, headaches and other stress-related conditions.

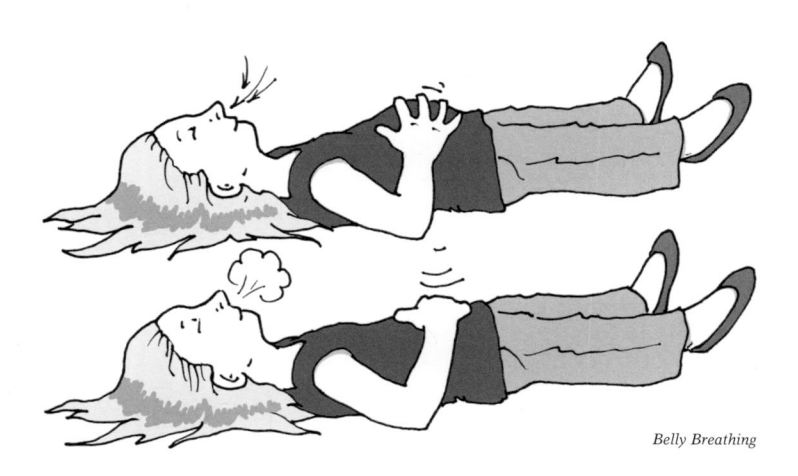

Belly Breathing

ACTIVITY · TIP #25 · VISUALIZE

Belly Breathing

Shake out all your tension and just let all the tightness in your body fall away. Make yourself comfortable. Close your eyes. Place both hands on your belly. Simply be aware of your breathing. Notice your belly rise when you breathe in (inhale), and fall when you let air out (exhale). Continue breathing through your nose, in and out. If you are having difficulty with this activity, try the following:

- ✓ Lie down and place a light weight, such as a book, on your belly so you can see and feel it rise and fall.

- ✓ Lie on your stomach. This position may make it easier for you to notice your belly rising and falling.

TIP #26 — VISUALIZE
Build awareness.

Feeling "nervous energy" or "butterflies in your stomach" is common before sports performance. Instead of trying to suppress this feeling to get rid of it, bring your awareness to it. Take a few deep breaths, or belly breaths, while you focus your attention on the "butterflies" in your body. By breathing into that area, you shift your mind to be present with the feelings and change how you experience them.

"When you can't center your eyes, you can't quiet your mind, and you need that quiet for your concentration—that's when the third eye (or the ability to visualize) comes into play."

Val Skinner
LPGA Golf Analyst, Former LPGA Professional Golfer

ACTIVITY • TIP #27 — **VISUALIZE**

Body Awareness

Find a quiet, comfortable place to lie down or sit. What do you feel? Do you feel any tingling or goose bumps? Do places in your body hurt? Just bring your attention to those parts of your body and notice what you feel. Bring your attention especially to any part of your body that seems to be calling you. Sometimes stomachs rumble, or toes tingle, or heads hurt. Just bringing your attention to your body parts helps decrease anxiety and concerns. Remember, there is no right or wrong way to visualize. Your way is the best way!

SEE IT. SAY IT. DO IT!

TIP #28 — DECLARE

Say It!

Say out loud what you want to happen; say it like it already has come true. In other words, start with the result and then work backward. A strong declaration transforms your attitudes and expectations in life. Practice declarations every day. Make cards or signs to remind yourself to say your declarations powerfully.

> "It's the repetition of affirmations that leads to belief. And once that belief becomes a deep conviction, things begin to happen."
>
> ***Muhammad Ali***
> *World Boxing Champion*

TIP #29 — DECLARE
Declarations are powerful — positive or negative!

Have you ever stood at bat, ready to hit? Your thoughts may be, "I hope I don't strike out," or "I'll probably mess up again." Remember, a strong declaration (or self-statement) transforms your attitudes and expectations in life, either positively or negatively! Positive declarations are powerful to counter negative self-beliefs or negative self-talk.

Your declaration is what moves you. It could be something like: "I am taking care of myself, physically and mentally," or "I am grateful for all support from my family, teammates and coaches."

Sport-specific declarations might include: "I am a strong batter," "I am quick and fast," or "I am steady and strong as I perform." Give yourself a gift... acknowledge who you are and reinforce this with positive declarations.

ACTIVITY **TIP #30** DECLARE

Get inspired

Create a chart of inspired declarations to help counter negative thoughts.

Start by making a list of your negative thoughts transformed by new declarations.

Start with "I am..."

NEGATIVE THOUGHTS	INSPIRED DECLARATIONS
I am a loser.	I am a winner.
I don't deserve to be here.	I belong here.
I am a klutz.	I am smooth and powerful.
I choke and mess up.	I take risks and play my best.
What if I blow it?	It's OK to make mistakes—this is a learning experience.
I don't want to let my coach or parents down.	My coach believes in me; I believe in myself.
I am stupid.	I am proud of myself.

SEE IT. SAY IT. DO IT.

TIP #31 — TAKE ACTION

Do It!

Successful businesses use action plans for their projects. A "To Do" list is not a detailed action plan, yet it does note things that need to be completed. The important part of the **Do It!** component is to first create a visualization, make a strong declaration and then take actions to make the project happen.

"I train myself mentally with visualization. The morning of a tournament, before I put my feet on the floor, I visualize myself making perfect runs with emphasis on technique, all the way through to what my personal best is in practice.... The more you work with this type of visualization, especially when you do it on a day-to-day basis, you'll actually begin to feel your muscles contracting at the appropriate times."

Camille Duvall-Hero
Waterski Champion

ACTIVITY TIP #32   TAKE ACTION

Action plan

See It. Say It. Do It!® Organize It! (Fishman, Dunnigan, Hellerstein, 2011) is a workbook created just for you! It contains organizational charts that you can adapt for yourself, your family or work colleagues.

Here is a sample action plan that I created for my first marathon, completed at the age of 57.

ACTION PLAN FOR LYNN

Seattle Rock & Roll Marathon—June 27

VISUALIZATION: Seeing myself cross the finish line, with my hands raised high, my body feeling good, a big smile on my face, hugging my daughter at the end. Gratitude and relief!

DECLARATION: I AM a marathoner!

ACTIVITY	START DATE
Visualize and state declaration daily	2/15
Healthy diet, sleep	2/15
Buy new running shoes	3/1
Start workouts in gym	3/1
Yoga 1/week	3/1
Weekly massage	3/1
Treadmill 3-4 miles on TWF March- April	3/2
Sundays- 7-10 mile walk	3/2
Appointment with podiatrist for orthotics	3/8
Increase walking 4-6 miles TWF May-June	4/15
Register for ½ marathon in Denver	4/15
Walk ½ marathon in Denver	5/15
Walk Seattle marathon	6/27
Celebrate!	6/27
Massage	6/28

SEE IT. SAY IT. DO IT!

TIP #33   TRANSFORMATION

Ta-Dah!

A Ta-Dah! moment is when goals are accomplished and dreams are realized. Transformation is about shifting from where you are now to where you would like to be. It is the process of taking continual steps in your life's journey. Acknowledge yourself and your teammates.

"Things come 'naturally' to kids when they have a clear mental picture of what they're trying to accomplish. Visualizing the shot, throw, swing, ball landing in the outfield grass, etc., gives their body a blueprint for success. As coaches, we spend hours teaching and reinforcing the physical parts of the game – we should also invest time with each kid to help create their own visual blueprints for success."

Dan Clemens
Coach and Author of A Perfect Season: A Coach's Journey to Learning, Competing, and Having Fun in Youth Baseball

TIP #34 Fears create obstacles and often stop us from moving forward in life.

Fears can terrify and even immobilize you. They may make you feel weak, helpless or frustrated. You may be fearful of looking stupid or failing, or even fearful of your own power and success. These feelings and behaviors are experienced by athletes of all ages.

When athletes are concerned with fears, they are focusing outside themselves. *See It. Say It. Do It!*® provides a way to address fears, empowering you to be a successful athlete!

"Be here now. Keeping your mind in the present moment is essential, as thinking about the past or the future takes your mind's focus away from your goal."

Craig Townsend
Sports Mind Training Mental Trainer

TIP #35 — It's never too early to start visualizing.

Even young kids can benefit from visualization. Young or older, the key is to practice DAILY—at home or at your sports activity.

- ✓ Visualize lots of detail: color, size, shape, form. The more detail, the more real the experience seems **(See It)**.

- ✓ Include other sensory systems, especially hearing and touching/feeling—even the smell of the surroundings.

- ✓ Include movement and body motion (running, walking, jumping).

- ✓ Imagine specific action sequences.

- ✓ Envision alternatives—if you falter, how do you recover?

- ✓ Be aware of things around you (people, field, lighting).

- ✓ State your declaration loudly and clearly **(Say It)**.

- ✓ Practice frequently **(Do It)**.

- ✓ Breathe/relax.

- ✓ Have fun! It's as easy as 1, 2, 3...

"The combination of solid physical training and confidence really comes together in sports. It's never too early to teach your child the basics of mental training. Training the mind is no different from training the body."

Alison Arnold, Ph.D.
*Mental Toughness Coach to USA Gymnastics,
USA Figure Skating, and six NCAA Teams*

ACTIVITY TIP #36 — VISUALIZATION

Script for ages 5-8

Parents or coaches can use this visualization for any sport. Modify it for the child's sport by substituting an appropriate exercise. This script demonstrates how a little imagination can help an athlete's performance.

PARENT TO CHILD: Stand with your feet together and jump with both feet as far as you can. Let's see how far you can go.

Child jumps. Mark the spot where she lands.

PARENT: Now let's do it again. But first imagine that you can jump farther.

Pause. Let her picture the mark you made where she landed, then see herself landing past it, and then your drawing the new mark.

PARENT: Now try it again.

Child jumps farther.

PARENT: It's like magic! Isn't that cool how your imagination can help you? Each time you have a new game or goal, remember how you can use your imagination and thoughts to help.

ACTIVITY **TIP #37** **VISUALIZATION**

Script for ages 9-13

PARENT: Find a relaxing place to sit or lie down. Breathe in and out *(pause)*. In and out. Gently close your eyes and allow your body to relax. Now, when you are ready, see yourself getting ready to play... *(whatever his sport is)*. Let's start by getting dressed. Put on your... *(guide him through his specific clothing, uniform, equipment)*. How do you feel?

Child responds.

PARENT: Go to... *(the gym, field, school—or wherever the athletic event will be)*. Imagine yourself looking strong, confident and ready to play. Take a look at the... *(field, court, etc.)*. How does it look?

Child responds.

PARENT: *Acknowledge child's response.* What is the weather like?

Child responds.

PARENT: Who else is there?

Child responds.

PARENT: How do you feel?

Child responds.

PARENT: Are you nervous?

CHILD: Yes. *Observe your child's response.*

PARENT: If yes, where do you feel nervous?

CHILD: In my tummy.

PARENT: Oh, that's very common. Just pay attention to your tummy. Try putting your hand on your tummy and breathe into your hand. Does that help?

CHILD: A little.

PARENT: That's OK. You can take anything you'd like with you in your imagination. Is there something you would like to bring with you to help you?

Child might want to bring a picture or small personal item.

TIP #38 VISUALIZATION
Sports preparation.

The first time you try imagery, it's helpful to have a skilled facilitator or practitioner walk you through the process. This is referred to as guided imagery. You can also use CDs, or record your own script to use as your guide. After you are comfortable with the technique, it's easy to practice these techniques on your own. The process is similar to the script in Tip #37.

ACTIVITY TIP #39 VISUALIZATION
Script for teens & adults

1. Sit in a comfortable place where you won't be interrupted.

2. Relax your body and take several long, slow breaths. Use belly breathing if you'd like.

3. Close your eyes and allow an image to appear of you doing your sport. This image can be one you've experienced or something new. It doesn't matter.

4. If you become distracted or find you are thinking about something else, simply acknowledge it and let it go.

5. Focus on your breathing if you lose the image.

6. Imagine the sights, sounds, tastes, feelings, and even smells of the experience.

7. Take note of as much detail through as many senses as possible. What are you wearing, who is there, what are you hearing, how do you feel?

8. Now allow yourself to go through the actual activity: dressing, arriving at the venue, gathering your equipment, warming up, getting ready to play.

9. Take your stance and go through the motion of your swing/run/hit/catch... see and feel every part of the activity, including the perfect alignment and the follow-through.

10. If you experience obstacles and fears (such as falling off the balance beam or striking out), imagine a time when you were very successful at the activity. Practice from that state of mind/body, when you were relaxed, having fun and performing well.

11. Continue breathing, relaxing and maintaining your awareness throughout the visualization.

12. Visualize success, completing your sports goal (crossing the finish line, hitting a home run, completing a routine...).

13. After you complete your mental practice, say your declaration (refer to sample declarations in Tip #30).

14. Use your declarations for support and confidence.

TIP #39

TIP #40 VISUALIZATION
Tricks to enhance your success.

If you find yourself falling asleep during visualization, you most likely are sleep deprived! Sitting up may be helpful.

Practice your visualization every day. This activity needs to be integrated and automatic for it to be useful during stressful times. Play back portions of the visualization sequence to develop consistency.

TIP #41 VISUALIZATION
Sports prep for a team.

Sports preparation starts with working on your own personal preparation. If you play on a team, next is to bring yourself—strong, powerful, and confident—to the team. If you're a coach, the next exercise is an example of using visualization with the team.

ACTIVITY • TIP #42 — **VISUALIZATION**

Script for a team

COACH: Think of a time when you and the team played a big match: when you were all working well together and everyone was on their game. Each played with power and focus, yet was relaxed. Imagine seeing and hearing your teammates. You are all super athletes playing together as one, supporting each other, and sharing the highs and the lows together. You help each other improve by knowing each other's strengths and weaknesses. You know you belong here, as part of a larger whole. Think of your team goals. Believe in each other. Have fun. Be proud of your team and your hard work together, trusting each other.

Now, think of a word, like "winner," that reminds you of the feelings, pictures, and sounds of teamwork and top performance you've just imagined. Say this word over and over again to bring you back to this team experience.

Write your word on paper and plaster copies of it all over your room. Say your word every day, at home and before practice. Know why you are here: to have fun, learn and work together. Ready? Let's break!

"My team's first game this season was against a team that we hadn't beaten for over five years. My captain had us close our eyes and imagine ourselves working together, building strong defensive walls, making the perfect hit to let our jammer out, racing out of the pack, catching back up to score points, and doing everything it would take to win the game. She let us focus on each scenario for a moment, imagining it and making it our own. At the end of it, I felt calm, centered, and completely capable. It was also a great moment of team connection. After that, we took the track feeling strong and ready, and sixty minutes of playtime later, we had beaten that other team for the first time in over five years."

Margot Atwell
Em Dash of Gotham Girls Roller Derby, Vice-Captain of Manhattan Mayhem and Member of the All-Stars Team

PART 3

PREVENTING INJURIES
VISION SAFETY

Is it okay to wear my regular glasses for sports?

What's the big deal about wearing protective sports glasses?

Many sports pose significant risk of eye injury. More than 40,000 sports-related eye injuries occur each year. The greatest number is in basketball, followed by baseball and then pool sports. Eye injuries may range from mild, like a slight scratch on the cornea (front surface of the eye), to serious and vision-threatening. After any injury, make sure you have your eyes/vision checked by an optometrist or ophthalmologist—even if you see 20/20! Better yet, be preventive.

TIP #43 Be Healthy!

The first step in improving visual skills for athletics is to make sure your eyes are healthy and your eyesight is good. The American Optometric Association recommends annual eye examinations until age 18 (starting at age 1, with InfantSEE® program) and then every other year after age 18. However, in case of any symptoms, injuries or concerns, eye examinations are recommended.

TIP #44 Use extra eye protection for higher risk sports.

An eye injury can impact your entire life, so wear safety glasses or shields for sports such as baseball, basketball, fencing, field hockey, football, ice hockey, lacrosse (men and women), racquet sports, soccer and water polo.

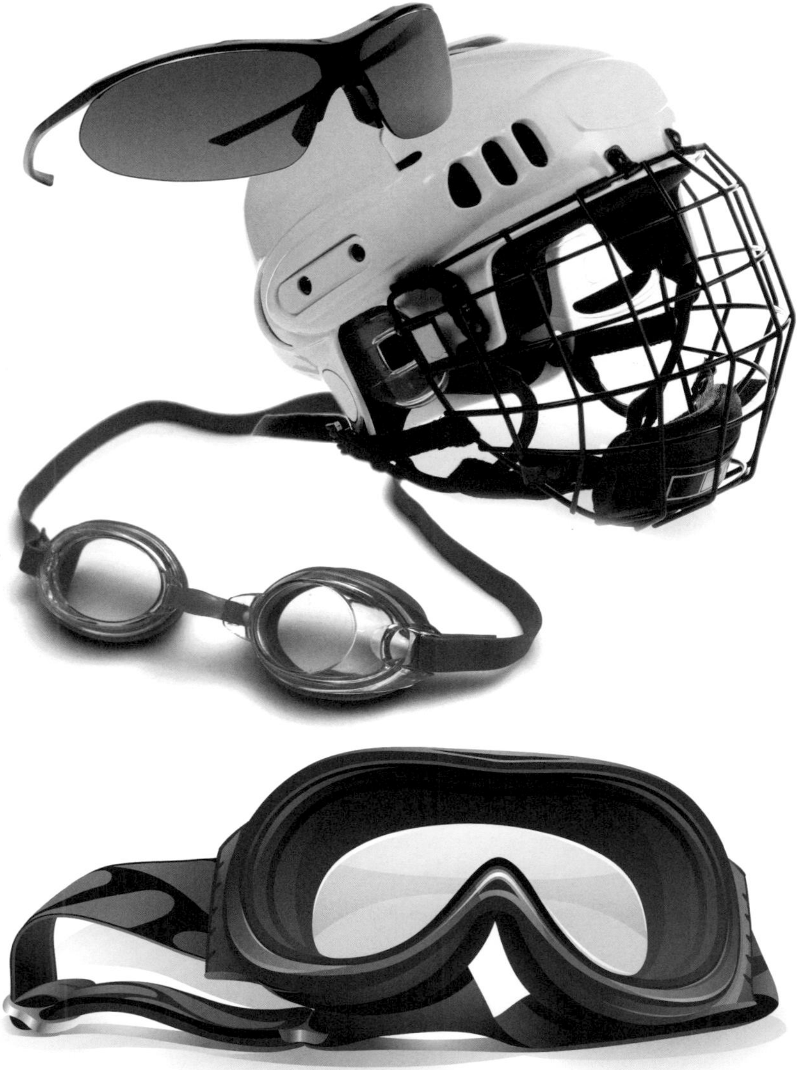

TIP #45 — Lens tints and sunglasses protect your eyes and can enhance your sport performance.

If you participate in outdoor sports and recreational activities, you need protection from the sun. Glare can interfere with your ability to see the detail necessary for successful performance. Tinted lenses can help. Tints transmit specific wavelengths of light based on the color, the amount of tinting and the lens material used. Guidelines can help you select the color tints recommended for your sport, such as neutral grays, yellow-brown, green, red, blue or polarized lenses. Tint selection is individualized for each person. Several companies have tinted glasses or products for specific sports. For more information about tinted lenses, see www.NeuChromaVision.com.

TIP #46 — Contact lenses may be a better choice than glasses for contact sports.

Depending on the sport, certain types of contact lenses may work better than others. But in some sports, contact lenses may cause problems because of a dusty or dry environment.

TIP #47 — LASIK refractive surgery may be a great treatment option.

LASIK surgery is highly successful in eliminating the need to wear glasses or contact lenses for sports. Yet some possible side effects could hinder your sports performance. Each person must weigh the chances for success versus risks. Talk to your eye doctor about whether you are a good candidate for refractive surgery.

TIP #48 Find an eye doctor you can trust and speak with about sports vision.

Many optometrists and ophthalmologists give excellent vision care. However, if you are really interested in an eye doctor to help you improve your sports performance, check out these websites:

www.COVD.org – Click on the "locate a doctor" link of the College of Optometrists in Vision Development (COVD) website. COVD Fellows are board certified in vision development and vision therapy.

www.AOA.org – Using the American Optometric Association's (AOA) "Find an Optometrist" search tool, you can locate an optometrist in your area who is a member of the association's Sports Vision Section.

TIP #49 — Practice, Practice, Practice...

Brain research shows that neurons that fire together wire together. In other words, when you practice, the nerves in the brain actually start networking and developing patterns so that movements become more automatic.

Consistency and practice are the key elements for success. Create a schedule for when you do your work, practice and play. Without structure, you may flounder and never get anything done. Then you are back to the frustration and struggles. What happens when you consistently practice the SEE IT. SAY IT. DO IT!® process? It's transformation time. **Ta-Dah!**

> "Practice makes...(not perfect).
> It makes PERMANENCE."
>
> ***Judy Willis, M.D.***
> *Neurologist and Educator*

TIP #50

Have Fun!

Find a sport you love and enjoy!

ABOUT THE AUTHOR

LYNN FISHMAN HELLERSTEIN
• • • O.D., FCOVD, FAAO • • •

As a pioneer in vision therapy for more than 30 years, developmental optometrist Dr. Lynn Hellerstein has inspired thousands to improve their vision and enhance their lives through her expertise and leadership. She has extensively used vision therapy with children and adults to treat learning problems, ADD, dyslexia, visual processing difficulties and brain injuries. She also works with athletes of all ages and all levels, helping them to enhance their sports performance.

Dr. Hellerstein is the founder of a private optometric practice in Greenwood Village, Colorado (Metro-Denver), with an emphasis in developmental optometry/vision therapy. She is a frequent lecturer and consultant nationally and internationally to educational, rehabilitation, therapy providers, sports teams and other medical/eye care professionals.

A Fellow of the College of Optometrists in Vision Development (COVD) and American Academy of Optometry (AAO), she is the Past-President of COVD. Dr. Hellerstein is an adjunct professor at several colleges of optometry throughout the United States. She is also a member of the American Optometric Association Sports Vision section.

To contact Dr. Hellerstein about presentations or workshops, call or email:

DrH@LynnHellerstein.com

303-850-9499

www.LynnHellerstein.com

To contact Hellerstein & Brenner Vision Center, P.C. about Sports Vision Training:

info@HBVision.net

7400 E. Orchard Road, Suite 175-S

Greenwood Village, CO 80111

303-850-9499

www.HBVision.net

Further explore Dr. Lynn F. Hellerstein's
SEE IT. SAY IT. DO IT!®
Multi-Award-Winning Series

SEE IT. SAY IT. DO IT!® products are designed for parents, teachers and kids to enhance visualization skills.

When visualization skills are increased, the resulting transformation creates success through school and life. It accelerates performance in sports, music and other activities. Confidence soars.

Dr. Lynn F. Hellerstein knows kids and vision. With her as your coach and guide, you will see remarkable improvements.

Available at LynnHellerstein.com
Please call 303-850-9499 about volume discount pricing.

SPONSORSHIP/PREMIUM OPPORTUNITIES

Learn how *50 Tips* can help your next promotional program:

- ✓ Gift-with-purchase
- ✓ Purchase-with purchase
- ✓ Available to major charities and national nonprofits
- ✓ Makes the perfect gift
- ✓ Small, easy to store and distribute
- ✓ Low cost, volume discounts
- ✓ High perceived value: help children and adult athletes succeed in sports and life, raise public awareness
- ✓ Easily customized—add your brand or event graphics to the cover
- ✓ Gain goodwill through association with other sponsoring charities
- ✓ Distribute valuable information to help athletes of all ages succeed in sports and life

For more information call

303-850-9499